VETERAN FAMILY IN CRISIS

The fight to save our home

Aria Maywood

PREFACE

Facts matter. The truth matters. As much as we want companies and people to do what is right over doing what's best for their earnings, that's just not the case today. The harsh reality is that you are nothing but an account number on a piece of paper or computer screen to banks, lenders, investors, etc. During these last three years of begging, pleading, and trying everything we possibly can to try and get our current and past lender to work with us and help us keep our home and avoid homelessness, one thing is perfectly clear. No matter how many times their representatives tell you that they aren't in the habit of taking homes, they actually are. How do I know this to be true beyond any doubt? Because this in May 2019, while calling in the second hardship forbearance payment to our current lender, the representative who took the call actually told me: "If we were in the habit of adjusting mortgages just to keep people in their homes, we would go broke."

This country has a growing poverty and homelessness issue, and I don't care what the governments stats and stories say. For us, here in LA county, all we have to do is take a drive around and we see the truth. States can shuffle and try and hide their homeless all they want, they still are human beings that exist in this world, and states and cities find it easier to cover and deny than to admit they don't have real solutions and options in place to solve and stop the crisis from getting any worse. In fact, the temporary solutions I have seen and followed, only manage to actually help and turn the lives around for a tiny handful of the expensive and deadly growing problem. So to hear the entity who literally holds your life (house) in their hands, and is the deciding factor in whether or not you get added to that homeless crisis or not, tell you that they would go broke working WITH homeowners and keeping them housed rather than foreclosing on those home, selling it for less, and adding to the increasingly costly homeless issue for that city and state, well I'm just sickened and mind blown.

Facts and the truth matter. Our facts and truths in a long and horrific three-year battle just to try and save our home from foreclosure and not be homeless, they matter. I made the mistake of thinking that somehow having a VA home loan (which the VA website clearly says "are the hardest to foreclose on.") would give us more protection and options if we bought our first home, than what we now know we actually have. In the event of a major life crisis or unexpected emergency, you actually are no different than any other mortgage debt holder in the country. It doesn't matter what branch you served in, how many years of service that you have under your belt, or what sacrifices or disabilities you get from having served, your home is a debt that must be paid.

In the event that you lose your job, have a medical emergency that leaves you drowning in medical bills you cant afford, that you face an emergency or tragedy that you neither asked for nor can afford, your mortgage still must be paid. You're an account number, nothing more. Today this is especially true, as layoffs and the pandemic have caused so much more additional and cruel hardships and losses for American families from one cost to the next. Getting by paycheck to paycheck is now the dream for most of us, one that we once lived happily in every day, content with just working our jobs and paying out bills. It isn't until your income is reduced or lost, and your ability to continue paying your debts is hindered, that you fully understand everything I am saying here. While I hope that you never have to go through what my family has for the last three years, if you do, you'll know that everything I say and reveal here and now is nothing but hardcore facts and truth.

The anger, frustration, disappointment and constant fears my family has been forced to endure for the last three years, is nothing unlike what hundreds if not hundreds of thousands of other homeowners have faced over the years, and will face soon enough. Unforeseen and unexpected serious hardships, emergencies, and losses lurking around the next corner which will throw you into the pit of despair like we were, and only then will you grasp the full extent of what we feel and are saying. For th last three years, my family has tried to survive and work through job loss, greed, health issues, and a growing pool of debt that had my husband's job not abruptly terminated his position four months after taking it, we wouldn't have in the first place. In the days and weeks and months before we were ever this far into the hole that we are trying to claw and pray our way out of, we were trying to get help, begging for help, trying to contact and share our problem with anyone who we thought might care and be able to help us. No matter how much I wrote or emailed or called anyone anywhere, we were never important to cover in the news or donate to our gofundme's or get any real kind of help just so that we could get back on track. Nothing. Nothing that is but the denial letters and excuses from the very people who had all the power and ability to help us when we needed them to the most.

So here we are, three years of fighting and trying to fight the lender (past and present) to help us and work with us so we can keep our home and not be homeless. And in just three months, with every option and ground to stand on having been used up and failed, we are most likely going to lose our home and be out on the street and nothing short of winning the lottery or a miracle is going to save us. Before this, I actually believed that good things happen to good happen, and in your darkest of moments, the light finds a way to shine on you and guide you home. But when your home is under attack by wealthy investors and lenders, protected so heavily by laws and money, you realize that the system always wins at any and all costs. Profits matter more than people, and playing the house flipping game is more beneficial to lenders than protecting and helping the families who turn those houses into homes.

Three months. Actually, less now that we're quickly coming upon the month of July. The current lender doesn't want us to tell our story, share the proof and facts that we have held, or talk about what we have gone through. They don't want others to know that you can stay and fight, that there are other options, any more than they want the government to be faced with the fact that there is a real problem in this country, and it costs more for states and cities to try and deal with and end the poverty and homeless crisis so many are struggling with, than if they pass legislation and laws that protect the homeowners and help keep them in their homes. In the coming months, more families are going to find themselves in our shoes, not because they are lazy or don't want to work or pay their bills, but because mass layoffs, health emergencies or other unforeseen hardships are going to be life changing events that they never asked for, and need this country to try and help and support rather than cast out and take from. That instead of trying to fix broken bones with little neon band aids, the hardworking American families, many of which have served this country honorably and now need help from the very government they answered the call to serve for, need to be fought for...need to be heard, needs to matter. To matter, at least as much as protecting the profits and portfolios of the investors, lenders and banks who hold the lives of these same people in their hands.

The lender wants me to not share our story, hardships, and this battle with anyone. They want us to quietly pack up and live on the streets while they sell the house for less than we bought and move on to the next loan they buy. Maybe I can't save my family by sharing our story and the chaos we've been facing head on for the last three, but if there is any chance that sharing this story might fall on ears that can help change things for others, that other families might read this and know that not only are they not alone but they do matter and can fight, if there is even the tiniest of chances that someone somewhere in this great big world can read this and maybe help be a lifesaving miracle, I have to try. This is my family, my home, and our story and lives matter. Families need things to change now, not later, and nothing will change if the banks, lenders and investors aren't held accountable for their choices and actions, especially when many receive hundreds of thousands of dollars to do just that, help homeowners keep their homes. This is our hellish story, and the battle for our home on Triton Ct.

PART ONE

"How it All Began"

There is always a moment in our lives, when we face difficult, cruel, or even horrific events and find ourselves saying or thinking, "If we had only known, we could have done something different." That is a repetitive thought that has lived in my mind for the last three years. There isn't a moment of any night or day when I'm not sick to my stomach trying to research anything that I could have missed, anything that we can still try and do, any options we haven't yet tried, or maybe there's some program out there we haven't tried to reach out to, just to try and save my family from being homeless and enduring any further suffering or stress. There just isn't. Time just seems to keep passing by quickly and no hint of even the smallest miracle or last minute saving grace, seems to exist for us.

In the last three years, we have had our hopes built up quite often, only to have them swiftly knocked down. It feels like the whole world is against us, hates us, or has chosen has us to punish for the problems and injustices of the entire world. I know that that can't possibly be the case, but that is just how it feels. Maybe I really was living in my own little fantasy world, thinking that with honesty, determination and proof of the wrongdoings against on our side, that justice would ring true and things would work out in our favor. At the end of the day, no matter how much you put into turning your house into a home, all it takes is one unforeseen disaster, emergency, job loss, or life changing event, to turn your world upside down and take it all away. And if like us, you make the mistake of thinking that somehow things will work out and turn around, you haven't yet realized that when it comes to mortgages and debts, you are nothing but an account number on a piece of paper, and that the laws are written to protect them and not you. That a simple computer program and calculators are the only things in this situation, that decide your worth and value. If the numbers don't add up, if It looks like you are more of risk to their profits and quotas, that's that.

Our lives were turned upside down and thrown onto this nightmare of a path, just four months after my husband left active duty to take his dream job and buying this house. Without any warning or justification (we still can't find a single reason for them to terminate his entire position!) he was just let go, called into the office informed he was done, and was escorted off the base like a criminal. A government job, with an amazing paycheck and benefits rival to that that we had had on active duty, we left the security and stability of active duty to take this job offer, and it was this paycheck that our mortgage payments were based on. Take home pay was easily around a thousand dollars a week, and for the first time in a very long time, it finally felt like things were going to turn around for us and finally we could stop worrying and going without, and just enjoy the rest of our time on this planet in our new home.

It was in august of 2014, that we closed on our home and held the keys tightly in our hands. Standing there in our front yard, planning out the numerous changes and things that we wanted to change or make, as the sound of school children at the nearby elementary school, echoed through the hot summer air. Having had a life of struggles and hardships, we never once spent a single dollar frivolously on anything that wasn't a have to have or necessity. Most people would have figured out their monthly bills and budgets and splurged on fancy new electronics, cars, or clothes.

Instead, we were creating a working budget to map out the mileage and gas budget needed to cover the two-hour drive (one way) to his new dream job, which he would now have to start to making twice a day, five days a week. It was a small and stressful sacrifice that we were willing to make, to give our son the chance to finally have the opportunities and stability he needed, that even while we were active duty, he just wasn't going to have.

We worked so hard in the year and months before we bought our home, getting our debts taken care of and working on increasing our credit scores high enough to even have the chance to get into our home.   Things felt good, for the first time in our lives, and it was so nice to go to sleep at night without worrying about much of anything. Life was good, until suddenly it wasn't. Fast forward to four months down the road, just before the holidays were upon us, and I will never forget the day my husband came home really early from work and had that ghost white and empty look on his face. After just four short months of making that four-hour roundtrip drive to and from his dream job, he was pulled into the office and informed he no longer had a job in that company and was escorted off the base like a criminal. I cannot even begin to imagine what he thought as they did so, or how humiliating it must have been.

It wasn't his fault, they still to this day haven't given him a valid reason as to why he was let go, and it's clear that we probably never will know. I don't know how many people have told both him and I that we should have hired a lawyer and sued for wrongful termination, but thanks to me, we didn't fight it and agreed to just let it go with our focus needing to be on trying to find a new job. That was our second mistake, with the first of course being taking the job that we knew was too good to be true but thought that maybe we were lucky enough to be getting a break from all the bad and tough. No, our second mistake was thinking that getting another job would be easier than what it ended up being. Fact time, when you are in your forties, have a sixty percent disability rating through the VA, and outside of the military your work history was limited and quite a while ago, getting someone to hire you was literally the most difficult thing my husband had had to do, including all of the tasks and things he did in the Marine corps and the Navy. Yes, my husband has dual service, and gave 4 years to this country in infantry for the USMC before he got out (that was long before he met me and my son!) and eight years with the US Navy, most of which was spent aboard the USS Carl Vinson. I remember watching him apply to every single job he could find, from sun up until sun down, even if it wasn't in his field or would barely be enough to help us to get by on. Phone calls, emails, gas to and from interviews that we somehow managed to scrounge together to pay for, one job application after another he filled out and turned in hoping something would pan out. Those dozens of applications quickly turned into hundreds, which soon turned into even more than that, as day after day we struggled to get by on just his disability check alone, for what ended up being a full year. Somehow, between the brief time on unemployment and his disability check, we managed to get by. Magically stretching nickels into dollars, and more often than not going down to one meal a day, usually dinner so no one would have to go to bed hungry. In that year after he was let go, we realized that we had now fallen below the poverty line, were now worse off than we were before he re-enlisted awhen my divorce from my son's father had left us without a roof, money, or much of anything outside of each other. I found myself having flashbacks to my childhood, where more often than not, we had our power and water shut off just so we could have food for the week, having to drive to the rest area nearby before school, so we could brush our teeth and get cleaned up before school, and how embarrassing it was that in such a small town everyone knew we so poor and always looked us differently. I also remember the happiness I was overcome with when I had my son, and the promise that I had made to him just minutes after he was born, that he would never have to go through or live as I had. I promised him that he was going to live a better life, and that I was never going to let him suffer or struggle the way that we did growing up. No matter how old he is, I intend to keep that promise.

During that year following the loss of our income, being unable to get hired anywhere, and me being denied disability (which we expected since most everyone gets denied their first time around) the only bills we were able to keep paid, was our mortgage, car, and monthly utilities. If not for the low income programs that many of the utilities offer, we probably would have been in trouble with them as well. There were so many days where we were down to eating once a day, I often went without just to make sure that my husband who was the only work capable adult in our home, and my son had enough energy and nutrition to get through each day. For the first time since I was young, I found myself actually having to get food from a local food pantry. The ladies who brought us food, were so amazing and hearing what we were going through, gave me a hug and said that things just had to get better soon for us. Honestly, I never thought that life could get any more difficult or low, as that point that we were in right then. Unfortunately, I was wrong. The sad truth in this crazy and mixed up world, is that as nice as it is to try and comfort someone with the idea that things can't get any worse, they always can. Shortly thereafter, life got a whole lot worse for us and pretty quickly too.

I need to make it clear since I haven't already, that we in fact did right away contact and tell the lender that had our mortgage at the time, what was going. We did our best to keep them updated as often as we could, even though we were making the payments on time and weren't missing any. That was partly because we knew that things weren't working out so well for us and we knew there were no guarantees. They didn't seem to care as long as the payments were made on time. They can never claim that we didn't inform of them from the very beginning, any more than they can try and claim we didn't beg and plead for help when we did start missing payments. For a full year after he became unemployed, we never missed a payment nor was the mortgage at risk, even with everything else in our lives starting to crumble. We busted our butts every day trying to make sure that kept the house safe from what we are fighting now, because it's all we had, it's what we worked so hard to get into and turn into our home. The bills that we couldn't pay, really began to pile up. By November 2017, we made the final mortgage payment that we could manage to pay, and now would have the month to figure out how to come up with the December payment. A family member stepped up, and helped us out by making that December payment which gave us a little breathing room, and got us through the Christmas, but the January payment was smiling at us from the not so far off distance. The mortgage payment, if you can recall, was based on the income that we no longer had, and with the payment being just over seventeen hundred dollars a month, and our income consisting of just the twelve hundred dollar a month disability check that my husband got each month from the VA for his disability, there was no way we could make those payments, so we made the call once again to the lender to see what programs or options we were available to us. Being that we had never had a mortgage before, we had always lived in base housing, we had no idea what our rights were, what options were available, or even what the laws were if you were a disabled veteran, had bought your home while you were on active duty, and now found yourself in the position of having a mortgage that was too high for you to afford.

I know people see that mortgage payment and cringe, but we were bringing in a take home paycheck of one thousand dollars a week, so honestly paying just under two thousand dollars a month for a three bedroom, three full bathroom pool house in southern California was a steal. The house next door to ours just sold for over three hundred and ninety thousand dollars! So all things considered, for southern California, paying what we were was actually pretty good. It was just too high for us to be able to pay now that our income was reduced, and we knew that we knew no one who would be able to help us pay that even if we could come up with half of that each month. We needed the loan to be modified, even if for a year or two, just so that we could continue making payments and not be at risk for foreclosure. In a perfect world, that would be a simple thing to do. Today, it's so much more complicated than I had thought.

We didn't wait 'til the December was due, we knew it was so important to try and get help early on, to avoid losing the house. We called the lender, told them we were going to have a problem trying to make the next handful of payments, and needed to get some help and buy us some time to figure things out. I remember telling the representative, that we were not willing to lose the house and would do whatever they asked to keep it. She was nice, and explained that they would see what they could do, but that we needed to try and come up with the payments in the meantime, followed by what would happen if we fell more than just a few payments behind. I knew she had to inform us of those things, but it was so hard to hear. We knew that this was a serious issue, and never took it lightly not once.

There was nothing physically we could do, I had already been calling, posting, tweeting, and emailing anyone and everyone that I could find the contact info for, for help. I may not be good at a lot of things, but writing with passion and honesty has always been the one thing that all of my life I have been good at. There were a couple times when my husband was aboard the USS Carl Vinson, that I had to take my frustration and passion for justice and truth and use it to help right some wrongdoings that in one case actually pointed out that my husband did in fact have the one single point he needed to make the next rank which allowed him to-enlist for his second contract and keep us from going through what we are right now. When I can help anyone or change anything that can help others, I feel like I have value and a purpose. Knowing that people are struggling and suffering while the majority of the country does nothing, just never set well with me and probably never will.

The lender sent us a packet of questions and requests for documents and info so that they could get a clearer picture of what our options would be. In all these years of this nightmare, I can say with pride that it has never taken but one day for us to fill out these packets, find and scan and email the requested proofs and documents they requested. They let us know that once that packet was deemed as "complete" it would take thirty days at the very least to review and determine what if any options they could offer us. We played the back and forth game, they never received some of the documents we sent them (research has shown that that is a common song and dance lenders do during loan modification attempts) but we had faith that they would come through for us and help us with a plan to save my family and help us keep our home. I continued my writing, calling, and social media campaign to try and drum up awareness to this issue and maybe if we were lucky, some help, but our family wasn't anything special and unless you have the right connections, more often than not your tweets and posts and emails fall on deaf ears and in the deleted bin.

Weeks passed quickly, and we sold off what little things we had of value, just to keep the lights on and our other utilities paid. Scouring the web for resources and programs that are specifically for veteran home owners, is enough to make your head spin. Seriously, I never understood how little there was in the way of resources and help for veterans facing and fighting foreclosures there really is. There are lots of programs for active duty, for veterans who have one hundred disability ratings, but nothing in the way of grants, scholarships, or programs to help veteran homeowners facing foreclosures or paying for legal fees to help you fight foreclosures. It's unreal! In a country that has sent its men and women off to fight and die in political wars and conflicts without much trouble, they sure don't put much interest or precedence in making sure that when those heroes come back as veterans, to have crucial safety net programs and resources in place to help them when they need this country to spring into action to protect and defend them when they need it the most.

I think it was then, that this system which my husband had given twelve years protecting and defending, really was broken and flawed. Designed to benefit and create more privileges and wealth for the already wealthy, which is why the programs and resources that have been in existence are underfunded and failing miserably. So much so, that, we have veterans dying waiting for appointments at hospitals, for mental health help, and because they can't deal with life turning its back on them or helping them when they need it the most. The very people who risked so much, who missed so many holidays and special moments while serving and protecting this country and its freedoms and people, seemingly stop having any value or matter once they take off that uniform. Veterans make up a good part of the homeless crisis that cities are struggling to address and solve, and these past several years, I can say that the veteran families I have crossed paths with have found themselves dealing with poverty and hardships that were due to medical emergencies they didn't plan on, job loss, car accident, death of their spouse, the list goes on and on and none of the reasons were their fault even slightly. They were and are just victims of a system that are most risk for poverty and homelessness.

By the time we were now three full months behind, reality had really set in. We hadn't received any help or options from the lender, I couldn't find any programs or resources that we qualified for to help us, and things just weren't getting any better. Once again it felt everything and everyone was against us again. There were no solutions or help in sight, I honestly thought about giving up and just walking away, I just wasn't sure that my nerves and health could take a dramatic fight to the death just to try and keep our house. Then, hearing my son swimming out in the pool late one night, beneath the clear star filled desert sky, I was reminded that this was the reason we bought this house and went down this road in the first place. To give my son who had so much loss and change that early in his life, a chance to have a better and happier future than what I had had growing up. I had to hold on and fight, we all did, for him. For us. We had worked hard and done what was asked of us, and this was ours.

It took March when the lender finally got back to us. What they offered us was a hardship forbearance, that would have us paying just 5.00 a month for six months. By quick look that's awesome when you don't have an income outside of the disability check each month, and barely can keep utilities on and food on the table. It began the first of April and would end September 1st. The terms were simple, don't ever miss a payment and don't pay late, and continue trying to get a job and increase our income. The representative we spoke with told us that at the end of this forbearance, if we need an extension, we would need to contact them and they would work with us. We were a little relieved, and had no reason to think that this was all they were ever going to do for us. She said this would stop all foreclosure proceedings in their place, and buy us some more time.

Each and every payment was made on time, as our bank statements can show, and we had no idea that while we relaxed a little and stressed a little less over the thought of losing our house, they were busy pushing forward with everything they said they wouldn't. The months flew by, and as we approached September, my husband still couldn't get anyone to hire him. I watched as his mental health and his physical health started to deteriorate. Eight years he had saved this family from the streets and poverty, which my son were facing after a nasty divorce from his father, and for those eight years he was the provider and money maker for our family. I can't imagine how hard it was for him to try and not feel like he was at fault somehow and he was failing us. None of this was his fault any more than it was mine. There was no way we could have seen things turning upside down on us. I've never blamed him for even a minute. We did everything tight, we were trying to fix the problems we were facing, we just couldn't find anyone to help us or give us a little break so that we could get ahead of this. Programs that I had been told about, were closed because the need couldn't compete with the federal grants they had had available, proving that things weren't actually going all that great for the working poor and extremely poor, funding was being shifted to walls and bailouts for wealthy corporations and the stock market, while veterans and working families struggle a little more every day.

The day I called in the final payment, I tried to get the representative I was dealing with, to explain what we needed to do about extending the forbearance. She stated there was no such thing, that all we could do was reapply for a review and see what they could do for us. That in fact, in July while we were making the on time and regular payments that we agreed to make, they had started the foreclosure process. (This is exactly why you HAVE to record your conversations and keep logs of names, dates, and id numbers of everyone you talk to. My stomach did a million flips all at once, and the panic started to set in. I was absolutely horrified!! We were flat out lied to, a huge lie, and I just couldn't believe it. My husband says this is why he has me deal with all this horrible and high stress stuff. While I may have a crippling nerve disease and an anxiety disorder, he has high blood pressure and PTSD that wouldn't react well with people and things like that. While I don't like dealing with it either, and being lied to is absolutely disgusting and shameful especially when you're dealing with matters like a mortgage, I get it. What I don't get, is how it was that that they could help us with the forbearance and explain that we had to do our duty to make sure the payments were on time and never missed and that the foreclosure process wouldn't be started or pushed through as long as we did, but while we were on it they go ahead and start the process for foreclosure. They lied to us about the extension, and they outright lied about them not starting the foreclosure process while we were in forbearance! They lied!! That phone call was the start of a seriously nasty and drawn out battle that we will never forget for as long as we live. I no longer wanted to deal with them in any form, and certainly would never trust anything they said any more. Shame.

Somehow, I managed to keep calm and civil, took a deep breath, and thanked her for the information and for taking our payment. She then explained, in a snotty tone, that we would have to fill out a new packet with them as we did before, and once we got it back to them, it would again take the same thirty days as before to look at and review to see if they could help us any further. they could offer us. It took them a full work week to mail us the new packet, but once again as soon as we got it, we filled it out and got it back to them just so we could sit, stress and wait some more. That waiting is so much worse than you can imagine when you're waiting for someone to decide if they are willing to do anything for you that essentially decides if you are going to be homeless on the streets or get to keep your home. The rest of September went by very slowly, and soon the holidays would upon us. October came and went, turning even more quickly into November. Since my husband came off active duty and we bought the house, we hadn't celebrated and still don't decorate or celebrate the holidays. Not a one of us had anything to be excited over, my son was now focused on his future that hinged upon us getting our housing issue solved so he knew he would have a home to live in while he went to college or made the decision to go into the military. It's hard to think about anything like that, when you know your mother and stepfather are suffering and struggling, and the first real home you have ever had is under threat to be taken by a lender who doesn't care about us or the house, they just cared about the loan. For me, all I could think about was the lies we had been told by the very company holding our house in their hands, and what kind of company not only lies about an extension but tells you that they won't start the foreclosure process while you're on the forbearance and does it anyways? The whole point of making the payments was to NOT face foreclosure during that time frame. What did I miss?

Just a short time before thanksgiving, we came to the conclusion that this lender not only had no intention of actually helping us at all, was dragging things out as much as they could on purpose, and had every intention of pushing the foreclosure through no matter what. They were not honest and were never going to represent our best interest nor help us in any way to keep out home. My husband and I decided at that point, that we had no chance but to hire a firm that would be honest and represent our rights and interests. Hopefully in doing that, we would not only show the lender we were serious about keeping the house, but that we were had no intention of letting them walk all over us and treat us less any longer.

The first firm that we hired (yes, as of today we have now had two), seemed to fall in our lap much like the dream job and house did. You have to make sure that you clearly express your situation, the outcome you need, and ask questions. I wish now that I had asked more questions than what we did, but we were so desperate and stressed out that we didn't want to waste any time. We had no idea what to expect, what legally we could do or was possible, all that we knew was that this lender was not honest, not helping us in any way, and it was beginning to take a toll on my health. On top of that, we were approaching one full year of missed payments, because once you're behind in payments, you have to pay the amount past due in full in order to reinstate your loan. Had it not been for that law firm, we honestly would not still have this house today.

We hired them right away, and at the very least, we no longer had to speak with the lender nor have any contact with them at all. That gave us some breathing room and allowed us to relax a little. Shortly after the firm sent the lender the typical paperwork that tells them we had hired them to represent us, had us fill out their loan modification packet, and started making regular contact with them, I have to say that I honestly thought this would resolve sooner than later and we could go back to being happy and living our lives. The lender, on the other hand, had other ideas. Back and forth conversations and updates, followed by a telephone conference with the lender, our lawyer, and my husband and I, seemed to make this lender uneasy and worried. I can't explain why I felt that way, but I did. Resubmitting papers we had already submitted, constantly battling the lender over how our printed bank statements weren't acceptable that we needed bank statements that they were used to, our firm began to realize we had been telling the truth and this lender was difficult and horrid. Things actually got worse!

I've now read so many horror stories of families who had to deal with their lenders claiming they didn't receive papers they did receive, sent things they never sent, and did all the unethical, shady, nasty little things they could to waste time and drag things out just so they could rack up the missed payments and charge the homeowners the various fees that they could charge. How our government lets them get away with that is beyond me! They don't even really hide it. In our case, we had just sent them yet another completed loan modification request packet, and they had marked it as complete on their end. This again meant that we would again have to wait the 30 plus days for them to go through and review everything to see what we could qualify for, except there we were in the very middle of our loan modification review period, and out of nowhere we get a letter from this nutcase lender stating that our loan had been sold off to the current lender and that they would no longer be servicing our mortgage!!! The letter stated that as of March 1sr, our current lender would be officially our new lender and that they were no longer responsible for our loan.

Our lawyer had no clue they even did it, at least not until I panicked and tried to explain to them as clearly as I could while crying hysterically. While yes mortgage lenders do that all the time, it meant that we would now have to start this whole process all over again. Which meant, that however long it took this new lender to get everything transferred over to them, review it, and setup our account with them, more months of missed payments and fees would continue to pile on. See, never say things can't get any worse, they most certainly can. As much as we hope and pray that the people who hold our homes, paychecks and jobs, credit and various loans in their hands are decent, caring, and honest entities, more often than not, they are not. They treat your loans and finances differently than you do, and care about profits and losses, not your best interest and wellbeing. Not your family and its future, not keeping you in your home and helping you get back on your feet. You are an account number, with the potential to make or cost them money, and that's it.

On a good note, this did mean that we were free from the previous lender, which yes we did the happy dance in our kitchen over that, but the idea that now we would have more high stress, depressing and sleepless nights ahead, and now had to start this horrible process all over again with someone new who had no idea about who we were or what we had been through, well something just didn't feel right at all.

PART TWO

"The nightmare Continues"

We knew nothing about the new lender, and because they had just taken over the loan, we literally had to start the entire process all over again. It was like we were stuck in a nightmare where the evil creature cast a spell and made us relive our worst nightmare over and over again as if it were the first time. As March 1st rolled around, we were now just about thirty thousand dollars behind. That means that our new lender had just bought an underwater VA mortgage, and new that it was a VA home loan and that we were really behind already. That much we know they knew.

Every night and day, I was still writing, posting, and tweeting our story and trying to find someone somewhere to help us. I just wasn't finding anything or anyone. Not even our pleas for help on our GoFundMe got us any attention. Life in this house was depressing, constantly worrying and stressing, and losing a little more faith in this life and people every passing day. It was too easy to turn our frustration and worries into arguments, every little thing suddenly seemed like big things. I blamed myself for this nightmare, and my husband clearly felt it was all his fault because he was the one who was the moneymaker and could take care of his family. Honestly, things just started feeling like this was all there was and nothing was going to work for us.

Every night before bed, I said a prayer (as I do now) that things will start to turn around, and somehow things will work out, we'll save our home, and this horrible nightmare will be over and lwe can find our laughter and smiles again. Maybe it was the prayers, maybe it was fate, whatever it is that you want to call it, my husband got offered an entry level job (with much lower pay than we needed to be ok) which he took right away. It was our hope that maybe by him working now, that more options would open to us through the lender. I guess part of me thought that they bought the mortgage because they thought they could help us. Maybe if I had had the mindset, that this was a profit and loss game and nothing more to these companies, it would have made a little more sense. I was getting us nowhere by assuming these companies and investors actually wanted to help people and ease some of the suffering and hardships they were going through.

The one thing that I think kept me fighting, outside of not wanting my family to be homeless and putting my son through that, was that the firm we had hired had made it clear that while there were no guarantees, we looked to be in good standing to get a modification which would reduce our monthly payments and possibly not have to deal with the missed payments at all. We were now so far behind now, that I honestly didn't believe there was anything left for us to do. It was starting to feel like the new lender only bought the loan because it was underwater and they knew that they could take it and sell it for a nice profit. This area is quiet and starting to grow, so with all the new homes going up and our location being one of the prime locations with easy access to shopping, schools, and highways, that just made the most sense.

Mentally, my husband was and currently is, exhausted. Our physical health has seriously been impacted with all this stress, worry, and depression as well. My husband made it through twelve years of military service without a single health problem, only to go through all that we now have and lead to him being diagnosed with high blood pressure shortly after this housing crisis started. We can't and probably won't get it under real control until we know our home is safe. Through now, I have tried so hard to be strong, not for me but for the dogs who don't deal well with stress or change, and of course for my husband and son. I figured if I try and hold it together, they will handle the ups and downs a little easier and for the most part, it has worked. We don't have much control over anything in this situation, and because everything seems to be protecting and behind the lenders, you just don't have that much to hold onto when you start to lose faith.

For the first time since this began, I honestly have to admit I was starting to give up and lose faith. We did get some good news after a little while, for the first time since we started to fall behind, it was suggested that we might need to file chapter thirteen to save our home.   We were trying to avoid that route, but knowing that we had that as an option did make us feel a little better. If anything, it gave us a little light at the end of a tunnel that had been dark and dreary for so long. You probably already know if you have been in this position yourself, but when you get this far behind, you dread answering the door, phone, or even getting the mail. Once they start the foreclosure process and file the default, you find in addition to dealing with trying to get the lender to help you instead of foreclose, you now also have to do with investors, real estate flippers, and all the scam artists who can see you're struggling and behind in payments and want to prey on you.

Having strangers taking pictures of the house at all hours of the day, calling you trying to get you to list your house with them, emails swearing that they can save your home guaranteed and get you your life, it just gets too much. You start to feel like you no longer have privacy or personal space, and that its already been decided that you've lost. It's such a horrible feeling. I watched as my son started shutting down and withdrawing from everything. He went from talking about college and starting his own life, to not really leaving his room except for food and if needed him for something. He broke my heart the night I peeked my head in and asked him if would start helping with things around the house now and then, and he responded with something along the lines of what was the point when e was just going to be living out on the street anyways. If you're a parent, you understand how heartbreaking it is to hear things like that.

He was just as afraid of his losing the only real home he had known after somehow making it through a nasty divorce between his dad and I and growing up with one military move and big change after another. It didn't help any that we had to also put his best friend that he had had since he was in diapers, to sleep due to complications of old age and some serious health issues. To have lived such a tough life and finally get to have your own room, garden to grow food in, and not have to worry about having to move any more, I get it. I guess having grown up in poverty and disappointment, I had just somehow become a little more immune to it, so had my husband. But that doesn't help me figure out how to help my son get through this, we shouldn't be going through it in the first place. And yet, here are.

By April 2019, the lender, after numerous months of stalling and countless denials, offered us a three-month forbearance plan that would have us paying just over fifteen hundred dollars a month, for those three designated months. It would begin April 1st 2019 and end on June 1st. The written agreement we had to sign, if we accepted it, stated that this was all they could do for us, which to us really meant that that was all they wanted to do for us. The firm was overjoyed and congratulated us, even saying that our worried and nightmare was finally over. I have no idea where they got that from, but maybe that was just me not bothering to get my hopes up again because it hasn't brought us anything good yet. If you read the wording in the agreement they sent over for us to sign and accept the terms, you would read exactly we did. Its written in a way that insinuates that after we make the three payments, they would give us a new payment and all would be well. It even spells out how much of a savings we would have over the next year with those payments. I think I read and reread the papers a dozen times to see if I was reading it wrong, but as our records can show, that's exactly how it was worded. As far as I could tell, this offer wasn't really anything close to actually helping us, it didn't nothing to help us work out a solution for the missed payments and definitely didn't reinstate the loan. As far as we were concerned, there was just nothing to celebrate.

The procedure for these payments were the same as before, each payment needed to be made on time and in full, no exceptions. When I was when I called in the second of the three payments, that everything became so much clearer. The representative took the payment over the phone, and when she asked if there was anything else she could do for me, I asked how long would we have to wait for them to come up with the new mortgage payment, going of course off of what the agreement we signed said, and she nastily flat out said that the only reason they put us on that forbearance, was so that we could have the time to get our income up, and that they had no intention of modifying our loan or helping us in any other way. That if we couldn't afford to buy and own a home we should have bought one that we could afford. Furthermore, if they got into the habit of helping every homeowner by modifying their loan so that they could afford it, just to keep their home, they would go broke! I lost it, can't remember what I said next honestly, I was too livid, but I hung up the phone and had to go sit outside to try and calm down before I had a heart attack.

By the time September 2019 rolled around, the firm we had been with could no longer help us any more than they did and they said our only option was to find a lawyer to file our lawsuit and look into bankruptcy. Unfortunately, because three years of missed payments had racked up, we no longer could in fact file chapter 13, because when they go in to break up the missed payments over the five years, it would be an additional one thousand and some odd dollars on top of having to pay our current mortgage payment and our income just didn't support that. After all of the fighting and trying to get help, we were now officially screwed. I lost it, had a total breakdown, cried until I was sick and exhausted. I was used to feeling disappointed, and I know what being afraid feels like, but nothing and I mean nothing could compare to what I was feeling right then and there.

I think I spent four hours, after everyone had gone to bed, searching all over the internet looking for something, anything, that I might have missed that could help us. I pulled our old GoFundMe and created a new one, trying to stick to just the facts of our story and struggle, and point out the urgency in our need to find someone to help us. I redid all of the email lists and contact pages I had made for all of the people who I had been writing and trying to contact before, to start sending pleas for help all over again. I was now in full panic mode, and wasn't sure what we were going to do. The problem was, nobody seemed to want to listen or cared. They still don't and after months of siting without a single donation, I deleted the fundraiser again and just created a new one. My days were and are now spent begging and pleading for help on social media. Why would anyone want to help us, there was nothing great or special about us. Once we were no longer active duty, we became invisible, and it really sucks.

My husband will disagree, but the reality is that first firm is the only reason we still are living in this house today. While they couldn't get the lender to be humane and actually help us, it is because of them, at least for a little while more, still had the house. In any case, the mission for us now, was to find a full service and affordable firm that not only could do loan modifications, but also handle the lawsuit that we needed to file. We managed to cross paths with the current law firm we are working, pretty quick. The lawsuit was carefully put together and sent off, and shortly after that, our attorney called us to tell us that the law firm representing the lender came back with a response to the suit. If we agreed to drop the lawsuit they would put together work with our lawyer to come up with an option for us.

This time, my husband was dead on right. Once we got a copy of the offer and agreement they wanted us to agree to, he was furious. I'm not sure what exactly we thought the lawsuit would do for us, but we had been led to believe that it was or best bargaining tool to save our house and now we have dropped it. Reading all the legal terms and conditions, it went on to state that by signing the agreement we would agree to drop the lawsuit and not pursue another one for the same issues. Literally everything that was laid out in the lawsuit, we had proof that they had said or done. The agreement then went on to address the NDA which I wasn't expecting but should have, after all, I had given our attorney every email and piece of documentation and mail that I had smartly saved since the beginning.

I have no doubt that they weren't happy with me sharing our story and struggles on the web, contacting congress members, and the various media outlets that I hadn't heard from but had sent off our story too trying to get help. It made them look bad, and could affect their business and profits. Heaven forbid they be held accountable for their actions! Unfortunately for them, the safety, wellbeing and happiness of my family, matters far than their comfort and profits. I have never hidden that I was and still am willing to do anything I can to try and get help and save our home. Lenders, banks, and investors always seem to find new and creative ways to skirt laws, hide violations and wrongdoings, and loopholes that homeowners just can't find or do.

Our lawyer explained that this was a good deal in the long run, and that we could still sue for whatever reason they give for denying us help. Of course we already know the reason, it's the debt and income problem. What it boils down to now, is that we owe almost seventy-five thousand dollars thanks to three years of drawn out stall tactics to rack up various fees, nonsense and countless excuses, denials and a clear refusal to actually work with us to keep our home. We were begging and pleading for help from the initial lender long before we were ever behind a single payment, when we knew things were going to be rough for a little while after my husband lost his job. They look at our income and debts, and see the three years of bills and collection accounts that we couldn't pay because we were paying on our mortgage and house and couldn't pay those as well. There is no way anyone could have foreseen things turning upside down for us like they did. By choosing to not help us, they helped to create the very reasons they list as being unable to help us. They seem to forget that we barely thirty thousand dollars behind when they took over the loan, and had we filed for chapter thirteen right then, we actually could have saved our home. That is totally on us but we had faith in our legal team.

First time home buyers, who have never really owned anything ever, much less had to worry about or deal with mess, don't know what their rights and options are. The mortgage holders, hold all the power and cards and therefore make the choices and decisions. They can choose to work with homeowners or they can choose to do a little that really doesn't the homeowner long term, and foreclose on the house so they can take the profits and start the process all over again. And now, here we are in the month of June. The lawsuit is gone, and suddenly it feels like we're battling to communicated with or lawyer, on top of not knowing what if anything there is left for us to do. I feel like this is over and we have already lost and no one wants to tell us. I mean seventy-five thousand dollars is a ton of money, money that we will never have, and unless we get that seventy-five thousand down to forty thousand which should put us in the parameters for being able to file chapter 13 and actually save our home, I don't see how there is anything left for us to do.

Honestly, I now can see why people choose to pick up what they can and just let the bank have the house. I guess if we had another to place to live and other options to ease the transition, we might have as well. It's so exhausting and sickening to have to watch the wealthy getting bailout after bailout, break after break, while the rest of us try to just hold onto the little we have. Try to keep our jobs, our homes, and our families safe and healthy. This isn't about even about our house, though having a roof over our heads is a basic necessity, no, fell in love with and wanted this house for the backyard. The spot for the fruit bearing trees, the in ground pool, the gazebo and raised food garden beds. Losing the house would mean not being able to take those things with us, and those silly things that mean so little too many, mean everything to my family. It was and is our little tiny piece of right and happy in this crazy world. I realize how ridiculous that sounds to some who might read this, but when you grow up in the dark and hard lives that we did, just having a tiny piece of beauty and serenity is everything.

For as far back as I can honestly remember, I have always hated the fact that we live in a country where some have so much, while so many more go without. You can work so hard to get something important like job to pay your bills, a house to keep you cool in the summer and warm in the winter, a working vehicle to get you to and from both and want nothing more than to just get by paycheck to paycheck and live your life, only for something out of your control to knock you down and let it all be taken away. The unexpected job loss followed by the year of being unable to even get a job at a minimum wage job, the piles of unpaid bills and collections, my god we never asked for any of it and we sure as heck have done absolutely everything we could to try and get help. Help that we couldn't get and constantly were denied for by not one but two lenders, even early on before things were so far along. When you follow the rules, do everything asked of you, trust people who should have your wellbeing and best interest at heart, when you write and call everyone that you can find to try and share your story with and try to find help, you have done everything you should have and could. The problem is that not everything nor everyone holds the same humanity, compassion, and human decency as the rest. Corporations and big and wealthy companies and firms care mostly about protecting their reputations and profits. It's far more beneficial to buy an underwater mortgage in a prime location for what you can get out of it and go after the poor and struggling homeowners for the difference and fees than it is to put them first and do everything you can to keep them in their home where they belong. I understand that, even if I don't agree with it. Some of us value the lives of the people around us and in our communities more than we do fancy expensive homes and cars. In a country that has so much wealth and prosperity, it is mind blowing that there is so much homelessness and poverty in our cities and states. Yet, there is.

We can't make the lender, any more than the lawyers can, decide to do what's right and help us. I can't magically come up with the winning the lottery numbers, and save us from any more tears and stress, losses and horrible injustices either. I can't make people buy the things I've made to try and create another income out of thin air (though I'm trying so hard!), any more than I can make them listen and really understand what the real problem is here. Cities and states, and the United States Government needs to pass legislation that protects American families, including its beloved veterans and their families, from losing their homes because an unforeseen emergency, job loss, hardship or life changing event happened to them and it's not their fault. Stepping up and helping the people before the wealthy companies and corporations should come first and be a no brainer, but it's not, so here we are. It's so stressful to not know what's going to happen next. And I have no faith that anyone is going to swoop in and help us. I'm absolutely terrified right now, disgusted, angry and seriously pissed off.

PART THREE

"Now What"

August 2014, while still on active duty, we bought this house, my husband started his dream job, and we thought that finally things were going to slow down and start working for us instead of against us. Life looked bright and good for us! We worked so hard to fix our credit just to get into the house, that it never dawned on that in just a short time, all that would have been for nothing. And now here we sit, getting ready to make the first payment on a three-month forbearance to a lender who for sure will not offer us any other option to help us keep our home. They know that we are irrelevant in the portfolio of mortgages they hold, and they know that they have the money, and laws on their side. They know, having now had three years of our bank statements and monthly expense documents sent to them, what our income is and that we can't afford the current mortgage payment as it is, on our reduced income, and they know they know that we can't afford to fight any longer. Maybe that is their tactic, to draw things out, make you so far behind that they know it would take an act of god or congress to save you, and that sooner than later you will be too desperate and down to hang on and cause a fuss.

I haven't given names nor any detailed information in our story, our truth. As much as I want to, to name and put faces to the people that are directly responsible for failing us, for causing us so much physical and mental harm, for the next three months we still have to make three more payments to them and pissing them off or giving them any ammunition to use against us wouldn't be a good thing right now. My family and I have been through a hell like nothing we have ever gone through before, and I wouldn't wish anything that we have endured on even my worst of enemies. My family is the most important thing to me, and keeping our home that we worked so hard to get into and make a home, it's part of that. I only have about a 1% bit of faith that somehow this will turn around. I mean stranger things have happened, just look at the high the other day of one of the coldest places on the planet! Still, I don't see a miracle coming our way. Besides, this forbearance gives us these three months to figure things out, I'm not sure what yet since we don't have the money nor place to go to, but you get what I mean. We aren't ready just yet to surrender our position in this war, and wave the white flag of surrender.

I feel the worst for the two shelter dogs that we saved the lives of a few years ago. Those two beautiful dogs were so badly abused and neglected, that they don't do well with change or stress and noises at all. Our male shepherd is the worst of the two, he lays on the floor shaking and shivering, with veterinary prescribed anxiety meds doing nothing to ease it, Benadryl barely taking the edge off, and just about everything you could possibly suggest right now, we've tried and found his ptsd is just too bad for them to work. We had a black Labrador when we first moved here, it was my son's childhood best friend. The two grew up together, and even when his health started to rapidly deteriorate that dog held on for my son who was dealing with his own internal crisis. We had no choice but to put him down and ease his suffering just a short time after we adopted the two shelter dogs. For the first time in their lives, you can see happiness and security in their eyes and faces, and for the first time they feel like they are home. They are safe, happy, and loved its true, but stable environments and homes are just as important to them as it to humans. Just thinking about putting these babies through any more stress or such a major change, will surely set them back and that just breaks my heart. I'm not sure either of them would last much longer after that. That's something that lawyers and bankers, lenders and investors don't care about but we do. If you have pets, you understand.

A few months ago, a good friend privately shared the story one of her friends, who is a military wife, with me. She told me, that her husband had died serving overseas, leaving her and small children to deal with the loss and try and figure out what to do and where to go from there. Her husband died serving this country, and she was facing foreclosure, as she tried so hard to get help from her lender, but they (like mine) were just as unwilling to do much of anything as well. My heart broke thinking about how much harder she had it with those young kids to keep safe and take care of, and she was getting the same excuses and runaround that we were. She was behind several months in mortgage payments, battling the VA for the benefits that surviving spouses are entitled to, and she wasn't getting the help she needed from her mortgage lender. It wasn't until she took to the local news station that luckily heard her struggle and story and gave her a public platform, that she was able to get any help. The difference between her and us, outside of her having more mouths to feed, was that her husband had been taken away from them, and on top of that loss and burying her soulmate, she was having to try and save their home and keep her babies fed! So, active duty and veteran families are facing the same hardships, losses, struggles, and injustices all across the country and they suffer and lose everything, only to matter when they are the faces you pass on your streets, or get annoyed with because they ask you for change. You are human before you are anything else, and no matter how much or how little money you have to your name, you have a purpose in this world and value, even if wealthy corporations, banks, lenders, and investors can't see it.

What's next? I honestly don't know. I'm on social media every day, on all the platforms that I have accounts on anyways, sharing our story and trying to raise awareness and maybe much needed help. But I have no idea what's going to happen next, and that scares the crap out of me. Before I was confident we could fight back, face off with the lender and get them to work with us. Now, after three years of crying, stressing, and watching them get away with dragging everything out all the whikle adding to the growing debt that clearly they know they will never be able to pay, I just don't know. All I can do is to continue to share our story, continue to tweet, post, and share our story and fundraisers, make and sell as much jewelry and art as I can, and pray. Pray that in three months we stumble across someone who hears our story and see this being a much bigger problem than just my family going through it, and can help us. At the very least, maybe by sharing and talking about our story and all that we have learned and been put through, maybe just maybe our story will comfort, inspire, others to take action.

FINAL THOUGHTS

I believe it was Gandhi who said something along the lines of how a nation can measure its greatness by how it treats its weakest members. This country has a long history of sending men and women off to political wars and conflicts, creating new waves of veterans, while continuously failing to provide them with the security, programs, benefits, and resources to deal with life once that uniform comes off. The families these same heroes have, have equal value, and ensuring that they are kept housed, fed, employed, and living healthy and long lives is the least we can do.

That is not how things have been or currently are today. Today we have numerous active duty families needing to rely on welfare to get through each month, veterans struggling with mental health and addiction problems that they aren't getting the proper access and resources to dealing with. Above that, we have veterans who are dying from hospitals not being able to treat or get them seen soon enough, and a growing number of veterans and veteran families are either currently living in their cars, on our streets, or thanks to the federal government not offering adequate and properly funded resources and programs, hundreds of thousands of veteran families are facing losing their homes, already lost their homes, and it shouldn't be this way.

These issues, food, housing, medical, and addiction treatment options, are essential to for our veterans, their families, and really all citizens in this country to live long, healthy and productive lives. Taking care of the men and women who time after time answer the call to serve, should never have to worry about coming home to evictions, homelessness, and poverty, but they are and do. With the rising number of layoffs, missed payments, unpaid debts, student loans, etc. we are paving the way for this nation to see a wave of poverty and suffering that could be avoided if we stopped putting profits above people and started focusing on protecting and taking care of our people.

These are not political issues, they are in fact humanity issues, and every family forced out of their home, every time a veteran dies waiting to get treatment or the mental health help they need, every time an active family has to go on welfare to take care of their family, we fail as a nation. Poverty and homelessness are on the rise with cities and states trying to find funding and permanent solutions while somehow wealthy corporations, banks and various other institutions get massive tax breaks, plush bailouts, and assistance. We've seen it for ourselves recently, as greedy and well-paid elected officials battle aggressively over crucial stimulus checks that should be enough to help save Americans who are severely struggling during this horrible pandemic, but barely flinch an eye when spending money on wealthy big business, industries, and the stock market.

Somehow, humanity and decency has been replaced by greed and political agendas, and the people who are dying, struggling and suffering aren't the wealthy. Something has to change, and it starts with each of us. If banks and lenders were held accountable for the loans they are fortunate to hold, and worked to keep families in their homes rather than focusing on the computer programs that decide profits and losses, we wouldn't be adding to our homeless problems and making mortgage payments affordable when the homeowners are victims of disasters, unforeseen job loss, or emergencies they had no control over, payments would be coming in monthly and prove they care more about the humans in those homes than they do their own greed.

It costs less in the long run, to have a nation of healthy, housed, fed and happy people than it does to continue the wealth divide, and fueling the growing problems that we can't afford to deal with. My family, like so many others across this country, don't want handouts or freebies. What we want, is to be able to work, raise our children, pay our bills and live our lives. Life happens. More often than not, we get sick, lose our jobs, get in accidents, suffer losses and have our lives turned upside down through no fault of our own. The faster that we get the opportunity and resources to get back on our feet, the less likely we drown in debts, face losing our homes, and have to watch our children suffer. If lenders and banks want to use the excuse that it would bankrupt them if they helped make mortgages affordable, then we need to put in their faces the cost of homelessness and poverty not just on our communities, but on our country as a whole. Unless your priorities are yachts, million dollar estates, and luxury cars, it would seem that investing in and helping the people that literally keep this country running is how you keep and increase the business of your companies and corporations.

My family, my home, my pets and food gardens are the most important things to me. There is nothing I wouldn't do nor endure to protect and provide for them. Since this whole house nightmare began, I have tried so hard to teach myself new techniques and try new creative outlets to try and create a second income so that maybe just maybe, if we are given the chance, we will make enough to satisfy the requirements for chapter 13 and can save our home. Unfortunately for me, handmade jewelry, abstract art, and digital prints and svg files are all things that so many others are making so sales are few and far between. The point is, I've been trying to do what the lenders have said we needed to. That being increasing our income. Between the pandemic and flooded market for the things that I know I can make, that's just not a simple task. Of course as you may have heard yourself, they always go to the typical "Don't you have family or friends who can help you?" For us, the answer is no. Just about everyone we know is struggling as well.

My question to them, since I never get an answer other than

increase your income, would be why can't you modify the loan even if for just a year so we can make our regular payments and then work on our missed payments? I honestly wish we could find a pro bono lawyer who would go after the first mortgage company who sold off our mortgage while we were in loan modification review, but we just don't have that kind of luck. In any case, if when we were only behind just a handful of payments, they had worked to help us modify or refinance or even add a second mortgage to our home we wouldn't be in this situation right now. That's the part that doesn't sit well with us at all... We were begging and pleading for help before we were even behind a single payment, we constantly let them know what was going on and our updates so they knew, they just didn't care.

I suppose it's easy to input numbers into a program and let it decide what's profitable and what's not, but that program doesn't have pets, children, or family to protect and provide for. I would rather spend the rest of my life paying for this house because we had to add what we owe to the back of the mortgage, than to keep sitting here night after night, sick to my stomach worrying about if we're going to lose our home in a few months. Sharing our story has helped some believe it or not, I know there will be those who will read it and have nothing nice to say, but in a roundabout way the people who could help us basically ordered me to shuttup while doing nothing to help us keep our home. The only reason they want me not to talk about it, is because they are worried that someone somewhere will read it or hear it, see the injustices that we've been forced to endure, (several of which were what was in our lawsuit) and help to right these wrongs. They are counting on us to give up and give in, and quietly go find a street to live on while they sell the house for far less than we paid or maybe they sell it for quite a bit more since we put in solar throughout the whole roof. It's no loss to them, and they can buy and take and sell the next family's home without a thought.

The problem is, I'm stubborn and tired of being beaten down and having things taken from us. If we break the laws, we're held accountable, and that should be the same for these wealthy mortgage holders. I made it worse when I googled the CEO of our lender, and the first thing that popped up was the story of how they had just purchased a multi-million-dollar estate. Seventy-five thousand dollars is what we owe to reinstate the loan and they live in an estate worth so much more than that. Hundreds of thousands of veterans and innocent men and women are living out on the streets or facing losing their homes like us, and they are living a luxurious life. Paid for by the mortgages and investments they have made. I wonder how many of us helped fund that estate.

Every day I scroll through and hear about stories of people who were suffering and struggling and somehow their story gets shared and crosses paths with someone who see the need to help and give second chances to those who need it. I've honestly written every nonprofit and organization that helps people in need, and of course with so many people needing help there just isn't enough funding to go around. Certainly none of them has the budget to pay off the missed payments and help us save our home and get our home out of the clutches of cruel profit driven lenders. It's hard to hold onto any hope, when we have for so long and nothing has changed for the better. I take that back, I found the courage somehow to write and publish our story which is one of the hardest things I have ever done. We've had a lifetime of hardships, struggles, bad luck and losses no matter what we do. We're so close to losing everything, there really isn't much that anyone can say or do to make us feel any worse. I have to hold on the hope that somehow this will turn out ok. If you can help people you come across, please do it without expecting anything in return, and just help them. If you can make a difference in even one person's life, give them the time and opportunity to restart life and get back on track, do it, not to post on social media for likes, but because it's what we need right now. Sometimes all some of us need is someone to see, hear, and understand and reach out a helping hand.

Two days ago we heard from our lawyer, and seems like the only options that we have left, are to give up and let them foreclose on the house, and try to survive on the streets, get as much of the seventy-five thousand down to fall within the parameters for us to be able to file chapter thirteen and save ourselves and our home, or win the lottery and pay off the seventy-five thousand dollars or house and put this entire horrible nightmare in our rearview mirror. We need a miracle, and outside of that we need immediate and change to the laws and practices this country has in place that continues to protect and help lenders, banks and investors while helping to add to the already unaffordable and growing poverty and homeless crisis. Something needs to change, and adding more struggling families to the homeless population isn't a positive change.

If you would like to help us work on starting this movement and raising awareness to the families and stories that aren't making it into the media, if you want to follow our story and updates or help us get the word out, please check out and save the links below. It would really mean the world to us. Thank you from the bottom of our hearts, for taking time to read our story, if you could keep us in your thoughts and prayers we would really appreciate it!

Follow, stay updated, and share our story and links!

Twitter: @KeepRVetsHoused
Facebook: https://www.facebook.com/keepourvetshoused/
Blog: https://www.keepourvetshoused.org/